INSTALLING LINUX

On A Dead Badger

(And Other Oddities)

Written by Lucy A. Snyder

and

Illustrated by DE Christman and Malcolm McClinton

INSTALLING LINUX

On A Dead Badger

(And Other Oddities)

Written by Lucy A. Snyder

and

Illustrated by DE Christman and Malcolm McClinton

Creative Guy Publishing

Installing Linux on a Dead Badger (and Other Oddities)

by Lucy A. Snyder
Illustrated by DE Christman and Malcolm McClinton

Published by Creative Guy Publishing.
www.creativeguypublishing.com
CGP-4014
ISBN-10: 1-894953-47-9
ISBN-13: 978-1-894953-47-4
October 2007
Trade edition

Cover design ©2007 Lucy A. Snyder
Cover and interior artwork (p.73) ©2007 Malcolm McClinton
Interior artwork (pp 14, 22, 26, 29, 30, 34, 39, 47, 51, 54, 61, 65, 97)
©2007 DE Christman.

The illustration on p. 22 incorporates incorporates Tux the Penguin, created by Larry Ewing; he writes "Permission to use and/or modify this image is granted provided you acknowledge me (lewing@isc.tamu.edu and The GIMP) if someone asks..." Mr. Ewing, please consider yourself heartily acknowledged, and warmly thanked.

Published in Canada.
Library and Archives Canada Cataloguing in Publication

Snyder, Lucy A., 1971-
    Installing Linux on a Dead Badger : (and Other Oddities) / Lucy A. Snyder.

ISBN 1-894953-47-9
    1. Computers--Humor. 2. Zombies--Humor. I. Title.

PN6231.E4S65 2007   813'.6   C2007-905004-2

All deft words are dedicated to Linux users around the world.

All daft words are dedicated to Everything's hot inner beauty.

All white space is dedicated to the eye of the beholder.

Table of Contents

Installing Linux on a Dead Badger: User's Notes

LET'S FACE IT: any script kiddie with a pair of pliers can put Red Hat on a Compaq, his mom's toaster, or even the family dog. But nothing earns you geek points like installing Linux on a dead badger. So if you really want to earn your wizard hat, just read the following instructions, and soon your friends will think you're slick as caffeinated soap.

Minimum Installation Requirements:
- one (1) pocketknife
- one (1) screwdriver, flathead, to install Duppy card (see item 4. below)
- one (1) computer with:
  - CD drive
  - USB, Ethernet, or a free slot for wireless networking card
  - Telnet or SSH client installed
  - cyberspiritual controller program such as FleshGolem (Mac OS X and Linux), Phranken (Windows 98, ME, 2000), or ItzaLive (Mac OS 8.1-9.x and Amiga)
- one (1) Duppy card (available in CardBus and PCI models) or SpiritInTheSky external adapter (available in ethernet and USB models)

- VüDü Linux (available from Twisted Faces Software)
- minimum 3' x 3' (1m x 1m) fireproof surface, in secure, ventilated area
- privacy
- one (1) dead badger, good condition

Optional Installation Requirements:

- one (1) gallon of holy water (*Bless!* brand exorcise water is ideal) in a silver or silver-plated bucket
- one (1) pair latex gloves
- one (1) fluid ounce of flea-killing shampoo such as *Ecto-Soothe* or *Mycodex*
- running water and a large sink or washtub

The following test installation was conducted on the concrete floor of the garage of a detached single-story house, on unconsecrated ground, using a 400MHz clamshell iBook, and began shortly after local sunset.

Step 1: Find a suitable badger. Specimens from zoos are ideal, but suitable badgers can be found as roadkill along highways in many parts of North America, the British Isles, continental Europe, Asia, and parts of Africa.

- Other animals of family *Mustelidae* and *Vombatidae* can be used in place of a badger, but an adapter may be required. See Appendix I for details.

Step 2: Once you have obtained a dead badger, check it carefully for structural damage, particularly in the spine, skull, and legs. Dead badgers do not heal, and a badger with broken legs will display limited mobility. Brain and spinal cord damage is likely to interfere with the Linux installation and render any successfully-installed system unstable, as well as voiding all explicit and implicit warranties according to the laws of any and every state, country, or alternate dimension, present or future.

- As a precaution against infection, wear latex gloves at all times when handling your dead badger. It is highly recommended that you wash the carcass with a suitable flea-killing shampoo.

Step 3: Obtain a copy of FleshGolem or other cyberspiritual controller program. This test was conducted with a copy of FleshGolem downloaded from the Apple site's utilities section. Follow all installation instructions carefully, including addenda in the readme.txt file.

- All cyberspiritual controllers should be compatible with either Duppy cards or SpiritInTheSky adapters.

Step 4: Insert Duppy card or attach external SpiritInTheSky adapter. Duppy cards work best if you're using a Mac with an Airport slot; response on the external SpiritInTheSky adapter may be sluggish. Further notes below apply only to Duppy card installation on the test iBook used.
- The card has a hinged lid and a clear cover over what looks like a small, shallow ivory box. Open and place a small amount of hair and blood from the badger in

the compartment, then close the cover, being careful not to let stray hairs stick out of the compartment. Install card into Airport slot by unlatching the small white tabs at the top of the keyboard, lifting keyboard assembly off (being careful of the wires), and inserting card into slot.

Step 5: Install Duppy card security antenna (included with card) in badger. Badgers may be run without security antennas, but this is not recommended. Insecure badgers may be hacked by anyone with a compatible card and badger bits. Each Duppy card/ antenna system is uniquely coded so that a properly installed system will allow only the original user to run the badger.

- To install antenna, make a small incision with the pocketknife at the nape of the badger's neck. Insert the antenna down the badger's back under the hide. Antenna must lie as flat as possible along the spine, or security will be suboptimal. Antenna may also be installed by cutting the badger's back skin open, but requires post-installation stitchery to restore structural integrity; this method is recommended for licensed taxidermists only.

Step 6: Install your badger's operating system. VüDü is the preferred Linux distribution for badgers and related species (see Step 1). This distro was designed by German software engineers who contributed to the SuSE project before they started up Twisted Faces Software in Jamaica. An alternative distribution is Pooka, which is available for download at

SoulForge.net. However, there is no alpha build for MacOS and Amiga, and some Windows NT users have found that the Harvey utilities built into Pooka may cause sudden, unpredictable invisibility issues.

VüDü Tech Tips

- Default partitioning: /root goes in the spinal cord and brain stem, /swap and /soul go on the left hemisphere of the brain, and /usr, /var, and /home go on the right. If you're working with a badger with damage to one of those areas, you can repartition one or the other brain hemisphere, but as noted in Step 2, using a brain-damaged badger is not recommended and may interfere with successful installation.

- System configuration information and the spiritual components of the package come on a small, rolled-up piece of parchment. Space is available to write in a password, as well as any auxiliary programs like NecroNull. The VüDü package comes with two scrolls, but a Santeria, Vodoun, Wiccan, or Catholic priest or priestess who has undergone Twisted Faces' scrollmaking training can also provide suitably blessed parchments. Check the VüDü home page to find a qualified cleric in your area.

- When modifying the scroll, be sure to use chicken blood-based ink, and write neatly. Various languages may be used on the scroll – VüDü is written in SoulScript, but successful modifications have been made in Latin, Hebrew, and Enochian. Further modifications can be made by Telnetting or SSHing into your badger later; start only with essential information. After finishing modifications, roll up the scroll and stick it down the badger's throat, all the way into the stomach. Use a screwdriver or pencil to get it all the way in.

Step 7: Install VüDü itself. In the package, there will be a large square of herb-scented paper. This is the entire code for VüDü. Fold this paper into an origami shape resembling the animal you're installing VüDü on (see also Appendix II). There are folding directions for common animals in the box. Make a hollow inside your paper badger and add a little more blood and hair from your animal.

- Don't lose the paper; replacements are expensive. There are recipes for homemade paper on the Web, but getting all the information correctly transcribed is a huge task, as this must be handwritten. Furthermore, the requirements of herb collecting, drying, and curing are formidable.

Step 8: Invocation/boot procedures. Place badger in center of fireproof surface, making sure ventilation is adequate and all doors are locked. Turn off all cell phones and pagers, and cease using all other unapproved electronic devices. Using the badger's blood, smear a foot-wide pentagram around its body. Place origami code-badger at the top point of pentagram, and light paper while making the boot incantation:

Suse vivo vixi victum reduco is ea id creatura absit
decessus a facultas Linux!
Dev root, dev root!

- The paper should burn with green flames. Black or gray means the herbs were improperly prepared. Purple flames indicate kernel panic; douse the flames with the bucket of holy water and abandon installation site immediately. Seek shelter at the nearest church or other consecrated area. You may need to enlist the assistance of an exorcist if you cannot reach shelter in time.

- When you produce green smoke, it should flow over the badger and into its mouth and nose. The badger will awaken as a Linux-powered zombie. Enjoy your new undead badger.

Common Problems

- Reanimation often results in animals that are in a highly aggressive, agitated state. It is highly recommended to have the computer close at hand during the incantation.

- If the badger isn't responding correctly, you may need to make some configuration adjustments via Telnet; instructions are in the VüDü manual.

- If the badger does not respond at all to the boot incantation, call Twisted Faces' tech support. Make sure to try all other troubleshooting options first. After two free calls, tech support will cost you an arm and a leg … and they'll only accept fresh, gangrene-free limbs.

DISCLAIMER: No badgers or Macintoshes were harmed in the course of this test installation. Your results may vary. Please note that zombie badgers are banned in California and Wisconsin; zombie badgers must remain leashed at all times in Texas. Zombie badgers can move at great speeds, and are prone to sudden acceleration; use proper caution when driving your zombie badger. Do not allow your zombie badger to consume mushrooms or African snakes, or your badger may emit catchy techno music. Do not taunt zombie badgers. Prolonged use of a zombie badger may cause acne, insomnia, leprosy, unusual weather, or the end of time. Please dispose of your zombie badgers properly; consult your local recycling company for proper disposal protocols.

Installing Linux on a Dead Badger: Appendix I

THE TECHNIQUES DESCRIBED in this article may be used to install Linux on various species of badgers; the following species are directly supported by Twisted Faces:

- American Badger, *Taxidea taxus*
- Honey Badger, *Mellivora capensis*
- Hog Badger, *Arctonyx collaris*
- Ferret Badgers, *Melogale* spp.
- Eurasian Badger, *Meles meles*
- Javan Stink Badger, *Mydaus javanensis*

With the aid of a WeezWhiz adapter (available from and supported solely by Handwavium Technologies), users may alternatively install Linux on other members of families Mustelidae and Vombatidae. Twisted Faces will not support installations on adapted animals:

- Northern River Otter, *Lontra Canadensis*
- Sea Otter, *Enhydra lutris*
- Maxwell's Otter, *Lutrogale perspicillata maxwelli*
- European Otter, *Lutra lutra*

- Giant Otter, *Pteronura brasiliensis*
- Tayra, *Eira barbara*
- Grisón, *Galictis* spp.
- Wolverine, *Gulo gulo*
- Striped Polecat, *Ictonyx striatus*
- Martens, *Martes* spp.
- Weasels, Ferrets, Minks, and Stoats, *Mustela* spp.
- Common Wombat, *Vombatus ursinus*
- Hairy-nosed Wombat, *Lasiorhinus* spp.

Linux may also be installed on metaphoric badgers with the aid of Handwavium's VüDü Doll series adapters. As above, Twisted Faces will not provide tech support in the event of problems. Handwavium provides limited support for installations on the following types of metaphoric badgers:

- small yappy dogs
- verbally demanding spouses
- Wisconsin natives
- non-native students, faculty and staff of the University of Wisconsin
- Tony Kaye, David Foster, Brian Parrish, Roy Dyke, Kim Gardner, Paul Pilnick, and Jackie Lomax

Please note that while zombie otters, weasels, and wombats are legal in some Wisconsin municipalities, actual and metaphoric zombie badgers are currently illegal to possess or create throughout the state. Combat wombats are illegal in Washington state. Human and spousal installation is widely forbidden throughout the U.S. Handwavium and Twisted Faces both state that they are not responsible for personal or spiritual difficulties arising from the use of their software or adapters in illegal installations.

Authorities Concerned Over Rise of Teen Linux Gangs

Boston, MA – On Friday evenings, scruffy bands of teenagers gather in alleys behind Micro Centers, Best Buys, and Apple Stores across the country. Going by names like "Team Mayhem" and "The Pipes," the Bawls-swigging teens trade Linux installation advice, brag about their video game prowess, and sneer at authorities.

"We're very concerned about what these kids are doing in their spare time," says FBI spokesman Mark Brasslathe. "Just a few years ago, they would have been safe in their parents' basements with their PlayStations, but cybermancy has changed all that. Now they're fast becoming a threat to the public welfare."

One young Linux gangster, who goes by the name "Retinoid," agrees that cyberspiritual technologies have radically changed the teen geek community.

"Two years ago, I installed Linux on my first dead badger," says Retinoid, who sports an orange Tux Penguin tee shirt that marks him as a member of The Pipes. "It was just wicked cool. We ran a warez FTP site off it and everything. But trying to run a game server on it was slower than an ice cream truck. So we

19

thought, why not make a badger network cluster for distributed processes?"

Retinoid and his friends were initially stumped when they couldn't find another badger.

"But then my kid sister's pet Chihuahua got killed by our neighbor's cat, and we were like, 'Why not?'" Retinoid says. "Turns out Linux will install on damn near anything as long as you know how to hack the code. We programmed little ChiChi to sing along to Kid Rock MP3s, and we took him with us to our next LAN party. Everyone loved it!"

Retinoid and gangmate "Pork_Sashimi" spent that summer building a redundant array of reanimated roadkill (RARR).

"The RARR was totally kick-ass," says Pork_Sashimi. "We had it serving up deathmatches and movies all day and night. Later on, we put an eyecam video interface on a dead possum, and we were able to remote control it into the ductwork of this sorority house down the street. Yeah, baby!"

Sixteen-year-old "DoomBarbie" says she met Pork_Sashimi in an online chat room. "He was all sexist and stuff, and he kept asking me to send him JPEGs of myself with my shirt off. He even traced my IP address and sent the Pussy Possum to my house. Can you believe it?

"But I totally got him back," she adds. "I hacked his possum and got some *very* funny QuickTime footage of his mom yelling at him about leaving dead animals in the garage."

DoomBarbie posted the footage on her Xanga site, fully expecting the war to escalate. "But then

Pork_Sashimi totally apologized to me! He admitted he got what he deserved and said he was sorry for acting like an idiot. How often does *that* happen on teh Intarweb?"

Impressed with her hacking skills, Pork_Sashimi recruited DoomBarbie for The Pipes. Her presence soon put a stop to their virtual voyeurism.

"It's not that I mind pr0n or anything," she says. "But they were all oohing and ahhing over this grainy-ass footage they got from a rat they sent into a strip bar, and I just started going off on the fake boobies. I was all like, 'That one's fake, and so's that one, and you can even see that *scar* on that one!' I guess it wasn't so much fun for them after that."

However, larger crimes loomed on their horizon when 23-year-old MIT dropout Dr. Hoonboi joined the group and took over as leader.

"The hackers love me 'cause they know that I can code," says Dr. Hoonboi. "These kids, they had all the potential, but they were wasting it 'til I came along."

Dr. Hoonboi declines to describe his group's exploits in any detail, but Agent Brasslathe makes serious allegations against the gang.

"We've linked them to incidents in Vermont in which FBI agents were attacked during Patriot Act investigations," Brasslathe says.

"Our agents were in the process of confiscating records from several libraries to determine which patrons have been reading works by Chuck Palahniuk, William Gibson, and other authors of terrorist-sympathizer literature," he says.

According to Brasslathe, agents were subduing the

librarians when several dozen squirrels burst out of the air conditioner vents. Some squirrels savaged the agents as others shredded records.

"Squirrels are much more vicious than most people realize," explains Brasslathe. "As a result of squirrel bites, two agents contracted Sumatran Rat Monkey Fever, which is evidently very common in zombified wild animals. The agents are still in a medical asylum awaiting brain transplants."

Children's librarian April Easley was preparing to read to a group of preschoolers when the FBI raided her workplace.

"These guys in suits came in demanding our circulation records, and we said, 'No way.' So then they pulled out the guns and the pepper spray. Sunny Saturday Storytime was *completely* ruined," she laments.

"They had our aide Bobby in a headlock and were wrestling him to the floor when the squirrels came out of nowhere. Those furry little critters completely sent the FBI guys to school. All us librarians were cheering, 'Yeah, go squirrels!'

"And the kids learned an important lesson that day: they may look cute and cuddly, but don't piss off a squirrel," Easley says.

"Next week our patrons are voting on a new library mascot, and I'm pretty sure Speedreader Squirrel is going to beat the pants off Benny the Bookworm," she says.

Brasslathe is upset that people like Easley view the zombie rodent attack as heroic. "Punks like this Dr. Hoonboi character are a threat to American freedom. Today he's interfering with terrorist investigations. Who knows what he might do tomorrow?"

Dr. Hoonboi denies having unleashed undead squirrels on the FBI.

"I'm much more a bunny man, myself," says Dr. Hoonboi. "If they have some real evidence, bring it on. Otherwise they should switch to a new brand of fertilizer. They're lucky I'm this totally centered Zen Master who's too busy being Zen to hire a lawyer."

Dr. Hoonboi gives a pep talk whenever The Pipes gather: "Before I discovered the truth in the dead badger, I was a child, and I sat in the dark playing with childish things. But Linux made me a man and opened my eyes to a bright, sunlit world of endless possibility."

"It is time," Dr. Hoonboi frequently tells The Pipes, "for the geek to inherit the Earth."

AUTHORITIES CONCERNED

Your Corporate Network And The Forces Of Darkness

New York, NY – Cybermancy is the hottest new trend in information technology. Companies worldwide are eagerly deploying cybermantic networking strategies to open doors to a whole new reality of profit.

"Is it a big deal? Absolutely," says Mindy Axedame, a top human resources specialist who consults for many Fortune 500 firms. "These technologies enable communication with the dead. That's *huge*. If a key employee drops dead from a heart attack, now you can ask him questions that would normally be lost to the grave," Axedame says.

"But it goes way beyond conference room Ouija – you can keep the dead employee on the job! Or truck in cadavers to raise for menial labor. One network tech can monitor and control up to twenty undead taking customer support calls – that's incredibly cost effective."

Axedame agrees that the technology provides staffing solutions that have yet to reach public acceptance or full legality. "Undead workers are kind of a gray area as far as the feds are concerned. And you bet your boots the unions are fighting it. But since you don't have to

pay the dead minimum wage, the potential impact this could have on America's bottom line is off the charts! We're pretty sure we can get the government on board as long as the GOP stays in charge."

She is quick to point out that cybermancy isn't just about turning corpses into tireless corporate assets. "These new technologies let companies interface their computers with some exciting extradimensional resources. Just last week, one of my clients hooked their systems up to the Cloud of the Ngartoleth – it's a hive mind that exists in a dimension adjacent to ours. The influx of new stock market prognostication enabled my client to cut his technical staff by over 30%."

Axedame says she anticipates networking with supernatural resources will save companies significant amounts of money.

"Oh, the prophecy these entities are giving out is

pure gold. My clients will be able to get rid of a lot of high-salary positions," she says. "Seriously, the Cloud just wants to be paid in live kittens. And kittens are a lot cheaper than full-time stock market analysts.

"Kittens are even cheaper than librarians! Who needs a company library when your computers are plugged into the minds of beings who control the darkest secrets of the universe?"

But with the blossoming of this new technological frontier, the physical and spiritual security of computer networks – and the people who work on them – has become crucial.

Professor Erwin Mandrake, head of the CIS department at Miskatonic University, is particularly concerned that companies are making rash networking decisions.

"Most people don't realize that even a simple Aetherweb LAN presents some truly dangerous challenges to IT staff," he says. "But Aetherweb with all its quirks and pitfalls is safe as a baby bunny compared to Ichornet."

Mandrake is particularly appalled over Ichornet's recent popularity. "It had 'Bad Idea' written all over it from Day One. I wish the companies who deployed it had bothered to check with experts first instead of just buying into shiny marketing."

Networking engineer Billy Winkler of Zerical, Inc., and his coworkers were looking forward to installing Ichornet.

"Hell, yeah, it seemed like a *great* product," he says from his hospital bed. "Deploying it's faster and simpler than setting up a wireless network, and it's light years easier than Ethernet. I mean, have you ever had to pull cable through an old building before? Pain in the ass.

"But with Ichornet," he says, "You just stick these little green eggs at key points around the building and they sprout and grow cables throughout the structure. We had our network up and running in less than six hours, with practically no effort on our part!"

Winkler says that within a week, issues with their new Ichornet arose. "Our help desk staff told us users were complaining that their computers were possessed by evil spirits. But the secretaries have *always* said that about our Windows machines, so we blew it off.

"But then, people started hearing scary voices ... you know, 'Get out or we'll feast on your rotting entrails.' Stuff like that. Five or six people ended up having to take psychiatric leave because of it. The rest of us, y'know, we just turned up the volume on our iPods and kept going."

"Things really went to hell when the cables didn't stay put in the walls. And when I say 'cables,' what I really mean is 'tentacles.' They broke into the plumbing. I hear the remaining staff don't wanna use the restrooms after what happened to me."

Winkler is reluctant to go into details about his accident. "I got grabbed when I was taking a leak. Gatorade bottles are in short supply at Zerical right now, if you know what I mean."

He is, however, willing to show visitors his lacerated left leg. When he pulls aside the bed sheet, one can see a large gash teeming with small tentacles above his knee. It spasms in synch with his heartbeat.

"Yeah, it's massively gross," he says. "The local

exorcist kept it from, y'know, taking over my body, but he couldn't get it healed up. The company's bringing in a Tibetan shaman; my doc seems pretty confident they can get me fixed up eventually."

He's pragmatic about the incident. "It could have been worse. At least it only grabbed my leg."

The Kronozon Corporation, maker of Ichornet,

insists that its product is not at fault.

"We've logged many support calls with these humans at Zerical," says the Mouth of Kronozon from the gates outside the corporate lair. "They clearly did not read the freakish manual.

"The network requires constant tokens of tender, fresh meats, but what did these humans do? They clogged its nutritional hub with canned animal sludge.

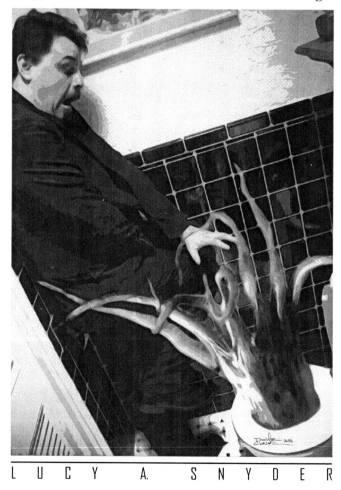

No wonder the poor network went into the plumbing – all that sodium made it thirsty! Foolish humans – no network can function properly under a load of Spam."

Lance Shriver, CEO of Zerical, regrets Winkler's accident. "We're doing all we can for him during this difficult time, and we're working to placate and secure the network in a cost-effective manner."

Shriver expresses confidence in the ability of his staff to resolve their Ichornet issues. "We have to fix it, because contractually there's no way we can replace it before next July. We're already behind on our major projects, and we have a responsibility to our shareholders to make a profit this year.

"We've given every employee holy water and a machete; past that, it's up to the individual to stay alert in their work environment."

Shriver agrees that they will switch to a less temperamental networking solution after their contract with Kronozon has expired.

"Right now, we're looking at Aetherweb," he says. "It's pretty much like regular Ethernet, but with all the cybermantic advantages we need to stay competitive."

Amanda O'Brien, a systems specialist at Monkeybrain Computing in San Francisco, is widely cited as an expert on debugging cyberspiritual LANs. She disagrees that Aetherweb is a straightforward networking solution.

"Sure, it installs just like old-fashioned Ethernet, lets you control your undead janitorial staff, and links your desktop to the All-Seeing Eye. All that and your proverbial side of fries," she says.

"But let me tell you, managing it is a major hassle. See, the unshielded cables give off this spiritual aura that's attractive to all kinds of heebie-jeebies from miles around. You have to get someone to bless the place or cast shielding wards, but there are always gaps in the coverage. Supernatural crap gets in here all the time.

"You know how when you pull the cover off your front-porch light there are all these dead bugs in it? That's what our network closets look like now. Only our 'bugs' aren't dead."

O'Brien recalls her early experiences with a shudder. "The faeries are the worst. I hate goddamned faeries."

She pulls up her shirt to reveal a rake of white scars. "A pixy did this to me. The other IT staff made fun of me at first, but then I was like, 'Okay, if you guys are such badasses, *you* try your mad ninja skills on the cute widdle faery. Just try.'

"They came back bleeding. Faeries will fuck you up sideways if you're not careful."

O'Brien has little fondness for any of the entities she's evicted from the network closets. "Trolls are almost as bad as faeries … not as dangerous, but three times as annoying. A troll gets into your network, it'll stay in there making a ruckus forever. I think the network emissions mess with their brains, because some of them just sound completely insane. There's no good way to get a troll out; you just have to wait until 6 p.m. and shut the whole damn network down until it gets bored and goes away."

Ever since the pixy incident, O'Brien has taken a practical, do-it-yourself approach to removing supernatural entities from the building.

"I don't think most of the popular warding services are a good idea from a security standpoint. I mean, does anyone really know *what* dimension the CEOs of these companies are from?"

O'Brien says that contingency planning is difficult because a networking tech never knows what he or she might find. However, she says that there are a few basic steps to ensure a good outcome in most situations.

"First, bug Human Resources until they agree to keep a priestess or witch on call, and keep her number handy.

"Second, always keep a heavy jacket and pants in your cube. Biker's leathers provide good protection, but so do Carhartts work clothes. And Carhartts won't suddenly become animated undead material if someone screws up the VüDü installation on a new zombloyee.

"Third, stock up on holy water, and keep a flask in your pocket. There is no such thing as too much holy water.

"Fourth, keep some fresh raw meat in the refrigerator at all times to use as daemon bait, and keep a stock of Little Debbie snack cakes for faery bait. Little Debbie is the bomb. Pixies like those angel food rolls with the cherry filling, and boggarts and gremlins like the peanut-butter-and-jelly oatmeal things. Just make sure the staff doesn't eat your stash.

"Fifth thing is you've got to keep containment devices around. Most faeries can be trapped in a coffee can – the iron immobilizes them. Just lure 'em out of the closet with a Little Debbie, slam the can over 'em,

slide a steel cookie sheet under it, duct tape the sheet to the can, and take 'em away. With daemons, you need to use real silver. We've got a sterling champagne bucket for the little imps that get in here sometimes. For anything bigger than that you've *got* to call for outside assistance anyway."

O'Brien stresses that the sixth step is perhaps the most important: always call for expert help if you've got a daemon of any size on the premises.

"We got a minion of Ghatanothoa in here when our network protections were still pretty spotty," she says.

"It would have killed everyone in the whole building – including me – if our new intern Mike hadn't thrown himself at the monster's feet.

"But you can't always count on having a suicidal virgin on staff who's willing to sacrifice himself like that. And you can't always count on a daemon being satisfied with just one virgin. So yeah. Keep a priest on speed-dial."

Faery Cats: The Cutest Killers

San Francisco, CA – From country homes to urban server farms, faery cats are taking America by storm as the hottest trend in pets.

Sixteen-year-old Melissa Eager's bedroom is decorated entirely with paintings and statuettes of winged cats, which she has acquired at science fiction conventions around the country.

"I love love *love* faery cats," says Eager. "And I had *no* idea they were for real until I saw one at a shop in Mill Valley. It was all black, and it had long, shiny wings like a raven. So pretty! I was all like, 'Mom, I will totally *die* if you don't get me that!'"

The purchase of the cat – a Balinese Sylphstalker named "Skynight" – was not an easy decision for Eager's mother, Victoria Knott.

"The shopkeeper wanted $2,500 for it. I could see paying that for a good handbag, but for a cat? I just wasn't sure.

"But Missy kept pestering me. And it occurred to me that if I bought her the cat, maybe she would stop spending so much time and money at those silly sci-fi conventions. I keep arranging dates with perfectly nice young men with good prospects, and then she goes to a convention and brings home these boys who spend all their time reading novels and playing games!

"So, I got Missy to agree that, if I got her the cat, no more conventions for her until she gets her business degree. At Harvard. If it keeps her on the proper path to success, then the cat has been a good investment," Knott says.

Exotic cat breeder Kyle Salinas says, "Faery cats have become extremely popular ever since the Shimmer Incident. Now that people can actually *see* the cats, they practically sell themselves."

Salinas says that faery cats – scientifically classified in the genus *Felis fae* – were created in Europe and Asia around 300 B.C. The cats thrived in Europe until the Dark Ages.

"Considering that plain old alley cats were hung for being minions of the Devil, you can imagine how superstitious folk reacted to faery cats, which in rare instances were the pets of various demons," says Salinas.

Most witches and wizards put an invisibility charm on their flying familiars to keep them safe. However, after the angry mobs caught the cats' masters, the spells remained unbroken and the familiars stayed invisible, as did their kittens.

Salinas says that, because of their invisibility, faery cats were left out of bestiaries and were often mistaken for other entities such as banshees, poltergeists, and boggarts.

"A faery cat in heat *does* sound very much like a banshee," he says. "And if an invisible kitten gets into

a house at night and finds a stash of catnip or valerian root, most residents would be convinced they need an exorcist."

The faery cats might have remained invisible to this day if it had not been for Angus Shimmer.

"It was totally an accident," says Shimmer, now

Associate Professor of Thaumaturgy at Miskatonic State. "I was in undergrad, and my quadmates were playing a practical joke on me. They'd stolen every last one of my spellbooks, turned them invisible, and had stashed them in trees around the dorms."

"Man, I was angry," says Shimmer. "And there was a storm coming – I was sure my books would all be ruined before I found them."

Shimmer says that he climbed the bell tower in order to cast a broad-range revisibility spell on the campus. Just as he was finishing his incantation, lightning struck the tower.

"We still aren't 100% sure what happened," Shimmer admits. "Maybe it was the copper in the bell tower combined with the moon phase and the power of the lightning strike and the hemiphasic alignment of Venus and Saturn – nobody knows. But at that moment, every invisible thing on the face of the planet became visible again."

In addition to surprises like the discovery of The Dunwich Horror in the back of a Waffle House in Tewksbury, MA, people across the world were shocked to discover faery cats living in their sheds and gardens.

"I had no clue these things were real," says artist Jim Beemer. "I mean, I don't even *like* cats, but I got tired of going to art shows and not selling a single piece while cutesy crayon drawings of crap-with-wings sold like hotcakes at the sci-fi conventions around the corner. So, yeah, I sold out. I'm not proud. I gotta pay off my art school loans somehow, right?

"But then I wake up one morning and there's this

freaking cat with wings on my patio. And it's munching on a freaking *leprechaun*. I check myself into the nuthouse that very afternoon but oh, no, they won't keep me, because I'm not hallucinating," says Beemer.

"Now even the collectors in SoHo want pictures of crap-with-wings. Nobody cares about my still-lifes or landscapes," he says. "That cat is out there every day, taunting me with his cutesy wings and his dead leprechauns. Haunting me. I'm haunted by a cat. God. The whole world's gone insane. I need a drink … where's my bourbon?"

Scottish faery fancier Edwina Cotton was also surprised by the flying felines.

"I kept finding the wee corpses o' pixies and brownies in me flowerbeds," she says. "I always thought it was me young nephew up to mischief with his slingshot, but it turned out I had a lovely fluttery tortie kitten living in me greenhouse."

"I brought the kit inside to keep her from slaughterin' the rest of me faeries," Cotton says, "but she's been quite a handful compared to me other cats!"

Salinas agrees that faery cats are much more challenging pets than regular housecats.

"Faery cats need space, high ceilings and places to roost. If you live in a small home, an outdoor aviary will do. But you can't just lock a faery cat in a parrot cage and expect it to do well," he says. "Most breeds will howl or refuse to eat under cramped conditions, but some from European lines can teleport short distances and will do so if they feel trapped. You can kiss your drapes goodbye if that happens."

He adds that not all pet owners realize that faery

cats were bred for a specific purpose.

"These creatures are beautiful and magical, sure. But their job is killing faeries. And if they can't do that job, they get frustrated and bored."

Cryptoveterinary researcher Rudy Briggs has spent several years tracking the origins of the faery cat. "We've managed to trace the European breeds to a Germanic witch named Scharlatte who had a serious problem with disgruntled pillywiggins tearing up her garden."

According to local legends, when the young cat she kept for mousing was able to catch a pillywiggin, Scharlatte hit upon the notion of crossing the cat and her pet crow to create an airborne hunter that could better catch the flittering faeries. After a few unsuccessful attempts, the cat gave birth to a litter of winged kittens that soon sent the pillywiggins packing.

"The crow-cat legend is similar to the legend of the Mandarin wizard Ming Mei, whose house was plagued by angry sylphs," says Briggs.

Ming Mei crossed his favorite cat – presumably a Siamese, according to Briggs – with a falcon. The winged kittens were fierce, quick hunters, and while they could not kill the sylphs, they drove the air spirits away.

"Many modern animal lovers are horrified that their kitties are bred to be merciless killing machines, but that's the breaks," says Briggs.

Faery cats have been increasingly finding homes as night guards in computer companies that have deployed cyberspiritual networks.

"The faery cats have been great for us," says

Amanda O'Brien, a systems specialist at Monkeybrain Computing in San Francisco. "We've been running Aetherweb for a while now, and the spiritual aura the network cables give off attract all sorts of supernatural entities. What the warding spells don't keep out, the cats take care of."

O'Brien says that her company's three faery cats – all Scotch Boggartharriers – have free run of the building.

"Yes, they shed just like regular cats, so we provide free antihistamines for people with allergies. Sometimes the cats will hork featherballs on people, but we've turned it into a positive thing for the staff. You get splatted with a featherball, you get the rest of the day off. So far – knock on wood – there haven't been any airborne litterbox accidents," she says.

O'Brien says that the staff reaction to the cats has mostly been positive. "A lot of geeks are cat lovers anyway, and our little bogie-slayers are real beauties. Pretty much anyone who would have had major issues with cats flying around resigned when we deployed the Aetherweb last year.

"Because, let's face it, if you can't deal with a cat sleeping on your monitor, you're going to be way less okay with finding a pillywiggin digging through your trash."

Dead Men Don't Need Coffee Breaks

Brooklyn, NY – Corporations across North America are eagerly embracing new necrotechnologies that enable them to employ the life-challenged.

"People are still a little uncomfortable with terms like 'animated corpse'," admits top HR consultant Mindy Axedame. "We prefer to refer to it simply as a kind of insourcing. We bring in the newly undeceased, which are an incredibly cost-effective resource for any company that needs non-managerial labor."

Rick Flint, CEO of the popular online discount retailer Hawt Shawpz, is thrilled with the new employment trend. "Just last year, our entire call center was alive. We had to pay each of those 200 people $7 or $8 an hour. And they wanted sick leave, and health benefits – it was nuts. We only netted 14 million last year; I can't afford frills and absenteeism."

But since Hawt Shawpz started insourcing the undeceased, Flint says, the company has become vastly more productive. "The dead don't call in sick or slack off on Fridays. They don't complain about rats in the walls. They're never late, because we bus them in from our corporate crypt. It's great! I can work a zombloyee for 20 hours straight for just $20 worth of pig brains."

Hawt Shawpz system administrator Brad Janett says that running the zombloyee staff is fairly simple. "I do the most work getting them booting Linux properly and debugging their wetware programming. The disk image gives them a hundred or so phone scripts to recite. Zombloyees are usually bright enough to pick the right script, even if they're not so good at forming words on their own."

Janett says that the zombloyee's cyberspiritual operating systems are extremely robust. "Pretty much the only problems we have are wetware failure. Mr. Flint thought we could do without air conditioning last summer, but then about a quarter of the call center mildewed."

Don Frites, owner of the O'Burger diner chain, says that life-challenged insourcing has been a boon to his company. He regrets that he can't use the undead as much as he'd like.

"Midwestern restaurant patrons have some squeamishness issues," says Frites. "They just aren't ready to accept a zombie taking their order or dishing up their chili. Zombies are great behind the scenes; you just have to make sure the public can't see them working."

Frites is quick to add that undead restaurant employees don't present any health risk to the public. "There's still this perception that they're these oozing corpses dropping parts everywhere, but that's completely outdated.

"When properly plasticized, our zombloyees are cleaner than our regular employees – all you do is wipe them down with orange cleaner every shift to get the grease residue off."

Ed Rudge, Outreach Director for Cybermantic Staffing Solutions Inc., sees a bright future for corporate insourcing.

"There's no limit to what businesses can do for their stockholders when employee living expenses are a thing of the past," he says. "Every one of our clients tells us the same thing: the dead are resurrecting corporate profit margins in a big way."

Business Insourcing Offers Life
After Death

Atlanta, GA – The zombie insourcing movement is revolutionizing the U.S. healthcare industry.

"Medical costs and insurance premiums have been rising 10-20% every year, and over 50 million consumers don't have health coverage" says Ed Rudge, Outreach Director for Cybermantic Staffing Solutions Inc. "That means that a whole lot of consumers are going to default on their medical bills.

"In the past, all an ethical doctor could do was to sell unpaid accounts to a collection agency. And a lot of doctors just aren't good at insisting on payment if the patient dies."

Rudge says that cybermancy has created solutions that benefit both families and the medical industry.

"When an uninsured patient is circling the drain, CSS pays a small fee to the hospital or attending physician so we can come in to speak to the families," he says.

"We show them their projected bill and tell them they have two options. First option is their loved one dies. Second option is they sign their loved ones to a post-mortem labor contract, the bill goes away, and they get to see their loved ones on Sundays.

"Our corporate priests visit the patient shortly before death and perform a ritual to download the soul and its memories into a duppy jar," says Rudge.

"We'll raise the body, preserve it, and install the operating system. The soul can express itself through the OS via our proprietary software. It gives the zombloyee and their family the sense that they still have an intact personality and free will, but our programming controls all their on-the-job behaviors."

Rudge explained that after a patient's corpse has been reanimated, CSS contracts with employers who pay $3-$4 per hour for the undead employee's work. Families get 15%, and the rest is divided between CSS and the physicians and hospitals that were owed money at the time of the patient's death.

"Most hospital-raised undead retain fair intelligence and motor skills, and we can work them 120 hours a week," Rudge says. "The Sunday reunions I see would just warm your heart. Most families are so thrilled to have their loved ones back they don't mind the way they smell one little bit."

Rudge estimates that most undead workers should be physically sound for ten years or so. "Hospitals tell us ten years is the magic number to get most bills paid off, so our cyberspiritual experts have been working hard to guarantee that our zombloyees will hold up under extended physical labor conditions. A call center drone should last much, much longer."

50-year-old CSS Contractee #1542A, who goes by the name "Chip," expressed dismay over his wife's decision to sign his corpse over to the company.

"I say, this zombie business ... utter bollocks," Chip says haltingly, taking a break from his 16-hour dishwashing shift to snack on a bucket of cow brains. "I was in a coma ... not dead yet! Now I'm in hot water all day ... this plastic skin bloody well itches. I want my solicitor ... can't work the phone. Gggggaaaargh."

Despite similar complaints of deceptive recruiting,

many terminally ill patients and people in dangerous lines of work are signing contracts with CSS and other labor supply companies.

"Hell yeah, I signed when the Infinity Labor guy visited our platoon," says Marine Corporal Lance Pike. Pike, a 19-year-old West Virginia native, says that Infinity has recently signed an exclusive contract with the Defense Department.

"He was offering us $10,000 sign-on bonuses," explains Pike. "I figure, shoot, my woman back home can sure use the cash, and if I take one for the team in Iraq, Infinity will get me back on the front lines with my buddies."

Pike's Infinity Labor recruiter, Rusty Tiburon, praises the young Marine's decision and hopes other servicemen and women will follow suit. "Now that we have the technology, it's downright un-American to just lay there and rot when you could be doing your part for the nation's economy."

Corporate Vampires Sink Teeth Into Business World

San Diego, CA – As corporations across North America embrace the life-challenged as cost-effective labor, many are turning to vampires to manage their newly-zombified staff.

"We always had a terrible time keeping our third shifts properly staffed and supervised," says Don Frites, owner of the O'Burger diner chain. "The new crop of vampires has been great. They're sharp, efficient, and we can partly pay them in cow blood from our affiliate slaughterhouses. Normally that stuff would just go right down the drain, and now it's keeping our night managers very happy."

Ed Rudge, Outreach Director for Cybermantic Staffing Solutions Inc. (CSS), says the corporate demand for vampires has increased nearly 1000% over the past year.

"Electricity is cheaper at night, so it makes sense for businesses to have third-shift zombloyee crews working factories and assembly lines, cleaning, trimming corporate lawns – the possibilities are endless," says Rudge.

"But zombloyees present unique management

challenges: they're not very bright, and they crave living flesh. Normal managers stand a good chance of having their heads cracked open when their z-crews get hungry. Vampires are in demand largely because they don't smell very good to the zombloyees. The z-crews listen to vampires instead of trying to figure out how to get to their sweet, juicy brains."

Financial analyst Bentley Chazworth says corporate vampirism is no passing fad.

"Let's face it, domestic zombie workers are cheaper than Chinese orphans. With a couple of buckets of cow brains and a vampire, you can run a windowless zombie call center around the clock. But you've *got* to have that vampire," he says.

"Unless you have a degree from a top school like Harvard, the job market's pretty tight for live workers," says Chazworth. "If you're a student in a state college MBA program someplace, becoming a vampire is definitely the way to go if you want a career in middle management."

Eve Hart, a night supervisor for a San Diego software firm, claims that CSS misled her during her recruitment.

"Sure, I'd heard horror stories of new vampires being sick for days, but CSS promised my transformation would be painless. I'd rate it right there with my root-canal, so … eh.

"But there was a lot of other stuff they should have told me about," she insists. "The sun thing, yeah, I knew about that, *everybody* knows that. I've always been sun-sensitive, so no biggie. But they told me my body would be practically maintenance free, and *that's* a load of crap.

"After a couple of days, I stank like spoiled blood. Ew. So I hopped in the shower, and I got totally burned all over! Nobody warned me about fresh running water.

"True, my period's gone – total yay – but I still have to shave my legs and get my hair cut. That's, like, totally maintenance-y."

When asked if she regrets becoming a vampire,

Hart admitted that she did not. "But I still feel like they weren't straight with me. And when my contract's up, if I ever see my counselor in a dark alley – well, dinner's on him, if you know what I mean."

Baron Olaf Würgerov says that he enjoys his newfound career as Overnight Overlord for the Hawt Shawpz customer fulfillment center.

"In olden days, I used to much enjoy putting villagers' heads on spikes," Baron Würgerov says. "I only sometimes get to do head spiking now, but you know, this job lets me assert myself in very positive way. I am much growing as person."

Baron Würgerov agrees that his transition from haunting subterranean Berlin to working for a U.S. corporation wasn't without a few snags.

"At weekly meetings, nobody want to sit next to me. It was all the rotted fluids, you see. After 1000 years living with rats, these little things you do not notice," Baron Würgerov shrugs. "So I learn about dry cleaning and Altoids. Is no big deal after all."

Business trainer Laura Loveblut, author of *Who Moved My Spleen?*, stresses that new vampires need to educate themselves to stay competitive.

"Knowing the ins and outs of being a modern corporate vampire is like knowing how to dress properly for an interview, knowing to send a thank-you note, or knowing that you shouldn't slaughter the secretary on your way out of the building. It's simply not your prospective employer's job to tell you these things," says Loveblut.

"Will you still have to shave? Will you still have to shower? Most definitely," she says. "Being undead doesn't mean you've left behind the expectations of the living world.

"You'll be able to see yourself just fine in any mirror, unless it's backed in real silver, and last time I checked Pottery Barn didn't stock many of those," says Loveblut.

"You *will* have to worry about burns from unusually clean running water or from water contaminated with trace silver. I tell my new vampire clients to invest in an elective ion exchange water filtration system for your home. It takes out the silver, and puts in just enough crematory ash to de-purify your supply. Braun makes a good model called Midnight Bathworks," she says. "And after you shower or shave, be sure to use a good moisturizer to prevent flaking.

"And kids, do yourself a favor: get those old silver fillings taken out of your teeth *before* you make an appointment with your campus vampire rep to have yourself turned."

Unemployed Playing Dead To Find Work

Columbus, OH – Some still-living workers have covertly joined the ranks of zombloyees in call centers and on work crews. Employment agencies have nicknamed these live workers "cryptos."

"I didn't set out to be a crypto, that's for sure," says a 33-year-old Columbus resident who identifies himself only as John. "I've got a BFA in musical theatre and an MA in Enochian literature; I always figured on being a college professor, but I got hella burned out in grad school."

John quit his PhD program just as Internet start-ups were discovering riches, and he quickly found work as a Web designer. However, his good job didn't last; the dot-com bust left him unemployed with no money to continue his schooling.

"I couldn't even get a job grilling weenies," he says. "Nobody's in a hurry to hire you for entry level work if you've got a graduate degree. They think you'll cut and run the moment you get something better. Which you will, but who expects anyone to make those jobs a career anyway?"

During his two-year unemployment, John made

ends meet by moving into a dilapidated farmhouse at the edge of the city with six dryads who had lost their forest to a failed condominium development. His parents also lent him money until his father was forced into early retirement.

"But then I finally I got a job at the Hawt Shawpz call center on the westside. Eight bucks an hour wasn't much, but it made my rent."

Disaster struck when Hawt Shawpz replaced their live call staff with zombloyees practically overnight. John was ineligible for unemployment, and soon his housemates were threatening to turn him into an elderberry bush if he didn't pay his share.

Despondent, John went to visit his elderly grandmother in her nursing home. "There was this cute girl there signing the old folks up for her zombloyee agency – I'm not gonna say which one. But listening to her ... the light just went on inside my head," John says.

"I chatted her up a little and asked what it would take for me to get onboard at one of the call centers," he says. "I haven't been eating too well and everyone says I look sickly, so I figured I could play dead pretty easily."

John says the young woman took pity on his situation and got him a copy of the call response script.

"I memorized it front to back – I was always good at that when I was doing theatre. We made this deal where I give her $50 out of each paycheck and she diverts the rest to my bank account; as far as their accountants know, the money's going to cover a private lawsuit that was filed against me before I died. The

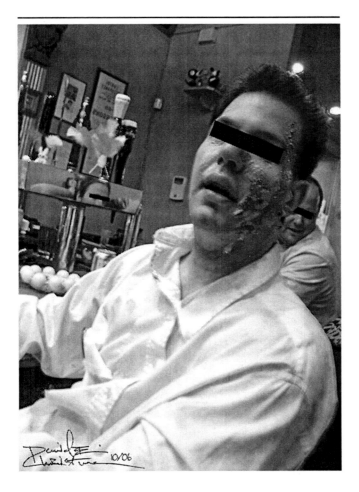

agency girl works things so I slip in and out on partial shift changes. That way, I don't have to work more than 16 hours at a stretch.

"I have to put this mix of rotten fish and catnip in my hair. The fish makes me smell dead, and zombies hate catnip. They won't come near my brains when I'm wearing that stuff, not as long as management feeds them on time, anyhow. Alley cats follow me home all the time now, though — the dryads are running a makeshift shelter for them under our porch.

"I work twice as long now to make what I did at Hawt Shawpz, and I have to wear a diaper because I can't take breaks, but at least I'm not homeless. Or shrubbery," he says.

John remains optimistic about his situation. "I'm getting really good at this zombie thing. I guess I'm a better actor than I ever gave myself credit for. If I don't end up joining these guys for real soon, I'm moving out to New York or LA to try to get some theatre gigs."

John's dryad roommate Ellora is confident that he will eventually reach his goals.

"He's pretty smart for a mortal," she admits. "My cousin's attached to a blue oak near FOX Studios, and she's heard they're going to start hosting auditions for a new reality game show called The Simple Unlife. They pitched it as cryptos versus celebrity vampires in Amish farm contests in rural Pennsylvania. John will be a shoo-in!"

Trolls Gone Wild

San Jose, CA – Programmer-turned-entrepreneur Frank Joseph has become one of the hottest Internet moguls with his unorthodox new video download service.

"Im in ur base billing ur doodz," jokes the 28-year-old Joseph. "Seriously, the cash is sick. Last month, I made more than what they were paying me for a whole year at Monkeybrain Computing."

Joseph says the first video was an accident. "My girlfriend had gotten me a new video camera for Valentine's Day, and I was just wandering around the company building on my lunch break trying it out. But then Amanda O'Brien called me over to help because she'd found a troll stuck in one of the network closets."

According to Joseph, the trapped troll appeared to be having a seizure of some kind.

"The thing was just flailing everywhere, wailing, gnashing its teeth. The network was messing with its head real bad, I guess. But it was so freaky, I totally had to videotape it for a little bit before I helped Amanda get it out of there."

Joseph uploaded the two-minute Quicktime clip

to his personal website so he could show it to a few friends. "But suddenly the clip was getting hit five, ten, thirty, then a hundred times an hour! I totally blew through my entire month's bandwidth limit overnight. And I'm like, 'Whoa, WTF!' you know?"

Joseph enlisted his coworker to help him solve the mystery of the clip's popularity.

"I traced the IP addresses in his server logs," says O'Brien. "We pretty quickly realized almost all the hits were coming from swamplands, caves, and urban wireless hotspots under bridges. Trolls."

Troll sociologist Brenda Moon speculates that the troll may have been in the throes of an orgasm. Or possibly it was railing against a proposed local gasoline tax increase.

"We're sure it's one or the other," says Moon. "I was able to translate words for 'fuel', 'Fascist', 'Ayn Rand' and 'masturbate'. It actually said 'masturbate' several times, so I'm leaning towards it having had a spontaneous orgasm due to Aetherweb emissions.

"Trolls find Ayn Rand very exciting," she adds.

Other experts disagree with her analysis. "Moon has clearly mistaken the troll for a member of *Truzlana urbanis*, but the purple spotting on its face marks it as a member of *Truzlana persisticus*," says cryptozoologist Jorge Billings. "The two species have different dialects with many homophones that do not share meanings in common. In the clip, the troll is saying 'What will the producers of *Star Trek: Voyager* do now that Tupac is dead?'

"Clearly, this is a very old troll," Billings adds.

Unconcerned with the meaning behind the troll's

shrieks, grunts, and groans, Joseph transferred the video to a secure server and started charging $5 per download.

"Some people told me I was wasting my time, but the trolls totally paid for it. So I set up a small, unshielded Aetherweb server in a self-storage place near my apartment to attract more trolls, started taking more videos, and it just kept going," he says. "I don't care what they're saying as long as the other trolls keep

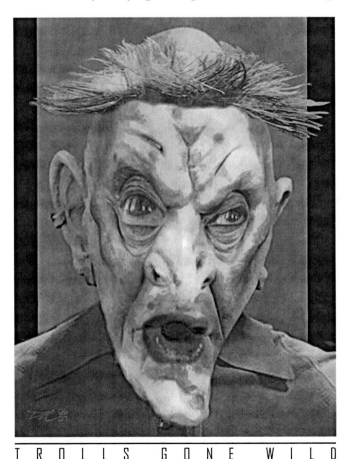

T R O L L S   G O N E   W I L D

buying it."

Within a few weeks, Joseph was able to set up his own Aetherweb-enhanced recording studio. Five months after he took the first video, he resigned from his job at Monkeybrain Computing.

O'Brien is pleased by Joseph's success. "Frank's a good guy, and he always brought in fresh glazed donuts on Fridays. But, honestly, he wasn't that good a coder; the new girl we hired after Frank left has been way better with PHP and SQL. So Frank's rich, our productivity is way up and Jenny got to quit being a crypto. It's a happy ending all the way around."

Not everyone shares O'Brien's cheerful assessment of Joseph's business. Some troll rights activists accuse him of harming and exploiting his video subjects.

"They look like they're in pain to me," says Kai Sunderland of Trolls Need Hugs Too. "I mean, okay, we can't prove that it's not sexual ecstasy, but it could be pain. And that would be bad."

The FBI reports that they're keeping a close eye on Joseph and his *Trolls Gone Wild* video empire.

"If he's harming these trolls, well, that's a local matter," says FBI spokesman Mark Brasslathe. "But if these videos are sexual in nature, and if any of these trolls turn out to be underage, you can be sure that we'll be bringing charges against Mr. Joseph. We take a very dim view of interstate smut peddlers, believe me."

Brasslathe says that Bureau pornography specialists are poring over the 100+ videos offered on Joseph's site. "We'll take firm, decisive action, just as soon as we can figure out what the heck we're looking at."

The Great VüDü Linux Teen
Zombie Massacree

BOB AND I ATTRACTED a pack of zombies when we stopped to fuel up and check our email at the Gas & Grep in Buffalo Springs. I hoped we'd lost them, but hope was all I had. Bob said they were the fresh remains of a high school football team who'd been drowned and de-souled by water daemons at a lakeside party.

Young, strong corpses have the speed and stamina to run down a deer. Until the sun and wind finally turned their flesh to stinky jerky, they'd be dangerous enough to make a vampire crap bats. And fresh zombies are persistent as porn site pop-up ads. If they take a fancy to the smell of your blood, they might track you for days, stopping only if live meat falls right in their laps

It'd be months before they got the Dead Man Shamble and could be taken out with a well-placed head shot. Of course, with the right software and hardware, you could kill even the most problem zombie, but that was some fairly arcane stuff, even for experienced hackers.

If my editor was right, Bob was one of only about five genuine cyberspiritual experts in the U.S. But so far he seemed more like a second-rate grease monkey than a computer guru. I had my doubts.

"Maybe we should go back to the Gas & Grep," I suggested. "Bubba said he had a sick badger in one of his pens. Wouldn't this work better with a fresh animal?"

More important, Bubba had plenty of guns and ammunition; all I had was a small 6-shot Beretta in the thigh pocket of my cargo pants. Bob had a small deer rifle in the gun rack of his cab. Not nearly enough firepower if the zombie teen squad showed up.

"'Taint no challenge, little lady," Bob said, his voice dripping with scorn and tobbaco juice. "Any fool with a copy o' Red Hat and a pair of pliers can put Linux on a live badger, or even a fresh-kilt one."

Bob hit a pothole, and I nearly lost my grip on my Treo PDA. My nice shiny new Nokia phone had fallen out of my pocket when the dead kid in the tattered Godsmack tee shirt was chasing me through the parking lot by the gas pumps, and I'd be damned if I was going to lose anything else on this trip.

I was going to kill my editor for sending me on this Texas Hellride. Absolutely kill her. Or at least demand a paid vacation. I could still hear Wendy's simpering wheedle: "The highway patrol says the Lubbock area is all clear; you'll be perfectly safe, Sarah."

Safe, my ass.

Bob was warming to his rant. "This zombie business is war. War, little lady, the kind Patton never dreamt of. We are fighting the gall-darned Forces o' Darkness. We gotta use some serious finesse, and there ain't nothing that spells finesse like installing a home defense system on a dead badger. You write that down, little lady. The readers o' *MacHac* need to know this stuff if they're gonna keep them an' theirs safe."

I dutifully typed it down on my Treo. I'd gotten pretty quick with the thumb keyboard, but as a precaution against being dropped in the mud I'd stuck the PDA down in a unlubricated clear polyurethane condom and tied off the open end with a rubber band. The condom, though dry, was still pretty slick, adding an extra layer of challenge to note-taking

"Hot damn, come to papa!" Bob abruptly swerved over onto the shoulder and slammed on the brakes. The Ford slewed to a stop in the caliche beside a stand of mesquites.

In the glow of the headlights was a dead badger, all four legs stiff in the air. It was on the large side, maybe close to twenty pounds. Bob hopped out of the truck and ran over to the badger, turning it over and feeling around in the blood-matted fur.

"The legs and spine and skull are in right fine shape," he yelled back to me, as excited as a ten-year-old on Christmas morning. "I can't feel nothing but some broke ribs. This'll do!"

He tossed the badger into the bed of the truck, and soon we were speeding back to Bob's shop.

Bob's Computer Shack was wedged in between a hair salon and a Subway sandwich shop in a little roadside strip. The big storefront windows on all the shops had been boarded up with plywood sheets and reinforced with two-by-fours and rebar; all the shopkeepers were relying on neon "Open" signs to tell passersby that they were carrying on with business in the face of the zombie apocalypse.

I followed Bob into the shop and he locked and barred the door behind us. The air smelled of dust and plastic with a faint metallic stink from a burned-out monitor he'd hauled in for parts. Soon, it was all going to reek of rotten badger. Bob carried the carcass over to a work table he'd already cleared off and covered with a long sheet of butcher paper. He wiped his hands off on his overalls and pulled out an old tangerine iBook, which he set on the other end of the table. I pulled out my Treo to take notes.

"Okay, first the easy crap: puttin' the Duppy card in the iBook so's we can get OSX to talk to the badger," Bob said. "I already downloaded a copy of FleshGolem from the Apple site – it's in the Utilities section."

Bob pulled what looked like a wireless notebook card out of a drawer of the table. It had a hinged lid and a clear cover over what looked like a small, shallow ivory box inlaid in the card.

"Next, you take some hair and blood from the critter and put them in this here compartment." He popped the cover open and smeared a hairy clot into the box.

Bob lifted the keyboard off the iBook to reveal the Airport slot. He slid the Duppy card inside, replaced the keyboard set the iBook aside.

I heard a thump and a shriek from the hair salon next door.

"Marla, git yer shotgun!" I heard a woman holler.

The woman sounded a little like Wendy, though the only time I'd ever really heard my editor scream was when a college intern lost an entire set of page proofs. Mostly she just took on a fakey-sweet patronizing tone when she thought you'd screwed up: "Well, we'll do this better next time, now won't we, Sarah?" She talked down to practically everyone like we were preschoolers. No wonder she'd been divorced twice.

Damn her for sending me out here. If I survived this, I was gonna demand vacation *and* a shiny new workstation.

"Okay, now we gotta install the Duppy security antenna," Bob said, apparently oblivious to the shouting next door. "You can run your badger without it, but it'd be pretty easy for someone to hack him if they could get some blood and hair offa it."

I jumped as the shotgun boomed twice in rapid succession next door. A chorus of zombies roared in pain.

"I told them they need a better lock on their back door," Bob grumbled. He got a penknife and made a small incision at the nape of the badger's neck. He picked up a long, thin, coppery wire and shoved it down into the incision like a mechanic forcing a rusty dipstick into a car engine. "You gotta get this to lay as flat on the spine as possible, or your security won't be good."

Now somebody was firing a pistol, the pops punctuating the zombie roars.

"Shouldn't we go see if they need help?" I asked.

"Those gals know how to handle themselves. Opening the door right now's kinda a bad idea."

He wiped his hands off and pulled out a bright yellow software box with a cartoon of a witch doctor on the cover. "Now we get to the fun part. We're gonna install VüDü; it's a wicked little Linux distro. If your badger's got some kinda brain damage, you can do a modified install, but it's a real bitch. And rabies makes the whole thing a crapshoot. Read the frickin' manual before you try it."

My heart bounced as dead fists hammered the plywood protecting the computer shop's front windows. I couldn't hear anything from next door; I hoped that meant the women inside had driven their attackers away.

"Don't pay that no nevermind; even if they got through the wood, they still got to get through the window bars. We got plenty o' time."

Bob pulled a small, rolled-up piece of parchment out of his desk. "This has the system config info, spiritual program components, and your password. You gotta write it all down on blessed parchment in something like Enochian or SoulScript. Write neatlike. Roll it up, and stick it down the badger's throat, all the way into the stomach." He demonstrated with the aid of a screwdriver.

The zombies were still hammering the plywood. A couple of them had found a loose edge and were wrenching one panel away from the bricks. One shoved a gray arm between the bars. The pane fractured and fragments shattered to the floor.

My hands were shaking too hard to take notes, so I set my Treo aside and dug my Beretta out of my thigh pocket. Not that I was in much condition to shoot straight, either.

"You ain't gonna need that yet," Bob said sharply, apparently irritated I'd stopped taking notes. "Them bars'll keep 'em back better than that little peashooter you got there."

I reluctantly stuck the pistol in my waistband and picked up the Treo.

He opened the VüDü box and pulled out an herb-scented scroll of paper. "This is the entire code behind VüDü. Fold it up into the shape of the critter, and put more blood and hair inside."

He unrolled the scroll and started folding it up into

an origami badgerlike shape. "It's real hard to make your own paper, so don't lose it. Open-source only takes you so far with this stuff."

The zombies had wrenched the first plywood sheet clean off the window. Three of them were growling and rattling the bars while the others hammered and yanked at the remaining boards. My stomach was twisting itself into an acidic knot; the bars really didn't look that sturdy. With every good pull, I could see the steel bolts in the cinderblocks giving, just a little. I wondered how far I'd get if I made a run for the back door.

I cursed Wendy a thousand ways. A vacation and new computer wouldn't even begin to make up for this trip.

Bob was studiously ignoring the zombies. Finished with the origami badger, he smeared a foot-wide pentagram on the paper using the badger's blood. He set the carcass at the top point, and put the origami badger in the middle.

"Now, burn the paper an' do your incantation." He got out his lighter, opened up the VüDü manual, and started chanting while he lit the paper. Bright green flames erupted, and the smoke curled around the badger's carcass. We watched as the smoke flowed into the badger's mouth and nose. It shuddered as it took a breath.

"We got badger!" He pulled out the tangerine iBook and started typing furiously.

The badger was trying to get up, its rigor-mortised legs jerking like Harryhausen stop-motion. It got its head up and growled at us, baring long canines. It sounded more like an angry grizzly bear; I didn't think something that small could generate such menace. I took a step back, just to be safe.

"An' that's why they call them badgers, little lady ... when they get mad, they're *real* bad news!" He laughed. "Nothin' pisses critters off like bein' woke from a good dirt nap."

I was feeling sicker by the minute. I'd had my doubts about the reanimation working, but it had never occurred to me that he wouldn't have the thing under control. The zombies had pulled the rest of the plywood off the window and were heaving hard on the creaking bars.

Bob opened a Telnet window and started tapping in commands. "Junkyard dogs ain't got nothin' on badgers. I seen a 15-pound badger send a 60-pound pit bull mix yelpin' and bleedin' back to his mamma. I mean, lookit the claws on this sucker. This bad boy could dig his way through highway pavement–"

The badger abruptly lurched to its feet and leaped on Bob, chomping down on his left forearm. Bob hollered and fell backwards into a table of disassembled PCs. The badger worried his arm furiously as it tore at his belly with its clawed forelegs.

I started forward to try to help Bob, but he waved me back frantically with his free hand.

"No! Git the iBook! Type in 'kill 665'!"

I did. The badger froze, still latched onto Bob's forearm. His tee shirt was soaked in blood from the deep slashes in his belly. He awkwardly shook his arm, but the badger wouldn't budge.

"Well that's a helluva system bug," he said weakly. "This little bastard's bit me right down to the bone. Launch FleshGolem, would ya? It's in the Dock."

I spotted a dock icon that looked like Frankenstein's Monster and clicked it. A program opened that looked a lot like the Mac port of the old *DOOM* first-person shooter game. Instead of a game screen there was a pixellated black-and-white image of Bob's face.

I was seeing through the dead badger's eyes.

"Cool," I whispered.

"Yeah, it's real cool, get this critter offa me! Hit the

'escape' key!"

The badger unclenched its jaws and fell to the floor with a heavy thump. The screen told me the badger was resetting itself. Bob clutched his bleeding arm, wincing. The badger righted itself and sat like a dog, awaiting new commands. The blood on Bob's shoes shone like tar through the eyecam screen.

"Dang, this stings," Bob said. "Where'd I put that medical kit, I gotta—"

The bars hit the pavement outside with a tremendous clanging crash. One zombie was pinned beneath the bars, but the other four poured in through the shattered window.

"Aw, dangit! Can't a man finish a presentation 'round here?"

Bob pulled a shotgun from a shelf beneath the work table and fired it at the rushing zombies. My ears rang from the boom. The blast hit the lead zombie squarely in its chest, but it barely slowed down.

"Git back an' get the badger running," Bob called loudly, apparently a bit deafened. "An' don't forget to initialize NecroNull in 'options', or he ain't gonna be much use."

Clutching the iBook, I ran to the back of the shop and spotted a closetlike restroom. I ran inside, flipped on the light, and locked the door behind me. The lock wouldn't hold for more than a minute or two, but I hoped Bob could keep the zombies busy long enough to figure out what I was doing.

Amid the roars and shotgun blasts, I set the iBook on the sink and moused around, trying to get the badger up and biting

While the basic controls were indeed fairly simple and *DOOM*like, there was menu after menu of advanced controls for a mind-boggling array of behaviors. There was even a Karaoke menu so that you could hook up a microphone and attempt to speak through the primitive vocal cords of the creature you'd reanimated.

Pushing aside the mental image of a frat boy drunkenly singing "Louie Louie" through a dead Pomeranian, I found the NecroNull combat option and clicked it on.

The eyecam screen shuddered and turned technicolor. A new menu of fighting commands popped up for regular Kombat mode and IKnowKungFu mode, the latter of which came with a warning that it was only good for five minutes before your golem spontaneously combusted.

My inner freshman giggled: *Spontaneous combustion? Fire is cool! Fire fire fire!*

I told my freshman to buzz off and set to kicking some zombie hiney in Kombat mode.

All I could see was a mass of legs, so I hopped the badger onto a nearby chair for a better view. Bob was leaping from table to table, trying to dodge the five zombies as he reloaded his shotgun. He'd blasted away parts of their limbs, heads, and bodies, but he'd only just slowed them down. Even the one who'd lost both its lower legs and all of one arm was hopping around on stumped thighs, gamely trying to grab Bob's ankles.

Bob turned his head toward the badger. "A little help here?" he called. His voice came through the iBook's speaker a half-second after I heard it through the door.

I leaped the badger onto Runs On Stumps. As the badger bit into the back of its neck, the zombie went rigid, and its skin went white and ashy. The zombie's NecroNulled flesh crumbled like clay beneath the badger's teeth and raking claws.

"Good one!" Bob said. "The others won't go so quick 'cause they ain't hurt so bad."

I attacked the next zombie, which had only a superficial shotgun wound to its shoulder. As the badger's teeth sank into its neck, the zombie roared and punched the badger into a pile of empty computer cases. I heard a dull snap from the speaker, and the badger shuddered.

The screen flashed:

WARNING! SPINAL TAP IN PROGRESS!
Kombat mode not possible.
Continue via IKnowKungFu? (Y/N)

Fire! Fire! Fire! my inner teen chanted.

I hit the "Y" key, and the screen went red. The badger rose up, up in the air and floated against the ceiling, scanning for targets. The zombie who'd fractured the badger's spine was flaking apart like asbestos, and the remaining three had cornered Bob, whose shotgun had apparently jammed.

Then Bob looked up, saw the badger, mouthed *Oh crap* and dropped to the floor, covering his head.

The badger screamed down on the zombies, jaws snapping and paws clawing faster than the computer could track. It went clear through one zombie's head like a fuzzy buzzsaw and ripped through the others. I caught a glimpse of Bob crawling desperately for cover at the back of the store. The badger dove in and out, faster and faster, like a small furry dead Superman.

WARNING! OVERLOAD IMMINENT!

I gave the iBook the four-finger salute, but the program was locked. I was just about to hit the power button when the badger exploded.

You know how matter can turn into energy? I found out later that the reason NecroNull is buried in FleshGolem's options is that when IKnowKungFu sparks a spiritual overload, it causes all of the still-living matter in the golem to become energy. A few bacterial cells, usually, or maybe a dying roundworm. Not enough to match the power of a nuclear weapon, but plenty to create one hell of a bang.

Is it a bug, or a feature? I guess it depends on how many zombies you have to kill, and how badly you want them gone.

The boom rocked the entire building, and I was knocked flat. The iBook clattered onto the dirty floor, its keyboard popping free and its screen blacking out.

I got to my feet and cautiously opened the door. Bob lay in an unconscious heap against the back door. The computer shop was a complete wreck. Smoke and zombie blood hung in a thick, rust-red mist. The remaining windows were shattered, and the front door had been blown off its hinges. There was not a single zombie in sight.

Two middle-aged women in pink beautician's

smocks stood on the sidewalk outside, squinting into the dark shop. One clutched a Mossberg shotgun. Though their faces and smocks were smudged with soot and blood, their bouffants were immaculate

"Are you okay in there?" the older of the two women called.

"I'm fine, but Bob needs an ambulance," I replied. "Does your shop have a phone?"

"Shore do. I'll go give the boys at 't VFD a holler," she said.

It took me three days to get back to civilization. I didn't end up killing my editor; when I got back we had what diplomats call "a frank and cordial exchange" and, well, we parted ways. After that, I did what any good American would do: I sued.

But all's well that ends well. I used my settlement proceeds to start up the Kritter Karaoke Klub, and the college kids can't get enough.

Wake Up Naked Monkey You're Going To Die

THE KETAMINE-LACED tranquilizer dart was wearing off. Jimbo raised his head, but all he could see were the glowing rainbow sprites swirling above him, moth-fluttering around the smoky oaky torches bolted to the cavern's ceiling. Pretty lights, oo, he'd love to float among them like a supernaut. If only he wasn't tied down to this rusty old sacrifice throne.

"Kill tone! Jelly smash!" yelled the Feeb.

The shout cut Jimbo's brain-haze like a razorblade on a punch-swollen eyelid. Thank God for ol' Feeb; he missed the Brainy Train all right, but what wits he was dealt never went dull, no matter how much booze or weed was in his system.

The Alleygat Autocrats had surely spat gigantic rainbows in all their minds, but Feeb, he knew how to keep everyone on course. A coarse, hoarse course, of course. Fuck him and the horse he coursed in on …

Jimbo's head fell sleepy-dead to his spattered chest.

"Explorers, come out and plaaaay!" screeched the Feeb.

"Wakey bakey," Jimbo snorted, his eyes popping open. He focused in on Bobby, who lay in a darkening pool of stickiness. The monster's minions had bobbed his legs clean off below the knee. A gummy machete lay mere feet away, just out of reach.

Fucking minions, Jimbo thought, his head clearing a bit more. What kind of nihilistic fuckclowns firebombed their own city and worshipped a big jiggly sonic death slug that wanted to apocalyze the whole planet? Big Slime could've promised to poop pure gold for all Jimbo knew, but who could cash it in if the world was cashed out? Stupid mooks.

Jimbo saw Bobby's chest rise and fall. His leg vessels had probably rolled up inside the stumps, saving him from a quick bleeding death so he could look forward to slowly melting in the belly of the beast.

Ain't life a peach? Always cut down, and not across, kids, Jimbo thought.

"Hey Bobby," Jimbo called, his throat dry and rough as the hemp ropes binding his wrists behind the wrought-iron throne. "Wake up, Bobby."

They'd crippled Bobby because he was the strong one, the one they couldn't rely on drugs and itchy ropes holding. Now Jimbo had to be Hercules. But first he had to bust free of this damned chair.

He craned his neck at the Feeb, who'd been strung up on meathooks through the flesh of his back in a suicide suspension. He'd survive, if they got him down and to a doctor before infection set in.

They were in a freaking charnel house; the greasy remains of countless bodies lay in festering puddles around them. Thank whatever God still cared about this pisspool of a city that their noses closed up shop soon after they found an entrance to the tunnels beneath the cathedral.

Hunt the Wumpus. Raise a rumpus, he wants to jump us ... crap, stay focused! he thought.

"Bobby! BOBBY!"

Bobby stirred and faintly laughed.

Jimbo knew Bobby was off bouncing in Happyfunball Land like he'd been. Still was. He had to give them both something to focus on.

"Bobby, did you know that Catholic priests can bless beer?" he asked. "They can even bless seismograph machines."

"You're shitting me," mumbled Bobby.

"No, I am being completely true with you. A Catholic priest could most especially bless that machete beside you, even though it's done you wrong, like that gal in that country song. You got no legs, Bobby, so don't try to walk, but get that blade and crawl over here with it. Bobby!"

"I got no legs?" Bobby started to drunkenly hum a Monty Python tune.

"Think of the nice blessed seismograph! 'St. Emidius, pray for us, and in the name of Jesus Christ of Nazareth, protect us and also this seismograph from the terror of earthquakes,' the nice priest says. Save us from the terror of singing puddings, Bobby Boy. You've *got* to."

"I can be abundingly Van Helsingly heroic now, Jimbo," Bobby replied, reaching for the machete. He gripped it, and started to king-snake forward, then went slack, his eyes glazed. "Pretty pretty blood, is it all mine?"

The Feeb wailed and fought his fleshhook chains.

W A K E   U P   N A K E D   M O N K E Y

"Ring ring ring the devil's calling! Come out, come out wherever you are!"

"Beer is life, Bobby! Bring the machete," Jimbo implored. "It's Miller time for sure! We gotta hump or we're skunked!"

A low, weirdly modulated rumble rolled from a nearby tunnel. It was the sound of a thousand pounds of ancient clotted slime dragging itself across the floor of the catacombs.

It was the sound of pure impending death, a sound older than evolution, a cosmic alarm clock blaring WAKE UP NAKED MONKEY YOU'RE GOING TO DIE! Every rat brain would fear it like the roar of an exploding star.

Jimbo saw Bobby's pupils expand as the adrenaline hit his blood, and suddenly Bobby was up on rawtorn hands and knees scrabbling to the back of Jimbo's chair, sawing at the knots. Jimbo felt the ropes give and he pulled his hands free, swinging his arms in a pitcher's windmill.

A Catholic priest could bless anything. A perfect, crystalline memory surfaced, lit by synaptic fire: the shutout game he'd pitched against St. Francis DeSales in high school. Their coach Father Santoro blessed his baseballs before the game: *May God guide your arm like he guided David's sling against Goliath, and with the Lord's help we're gonna beat the snot out of those rich little nancyboys at St. Francis. Amen.*

He felt in his pocket for their salvation: the aluminum jar of caustic salt was still there. The last priest alive in the city had blessed it. The minions didn't think to strip them of anything but obvious weapons. Stupid mooks.

The ancient acidic God Slime crawled into the flickering torchlight like an enormous, unholy pudding glistening with a million emerald eyes. It was humming, vibrating, getting louder. They only had a few susurrous heartbeats until it reached the deadly tone to batter bones and muscles to pulp, liquefying their flesh so the acidic abomination could sponge them into its hundred stomachs.

Jimbo pulled out the blessed jar and gripped it split-fingered for a fastball. He whispered, "Sing a song of sixpence, slimeball, 'cause I got a pocket full of lye!"

He wished to himself, prayed to God and pitched as hard as he could. The shiny jar hit the mark and sank fast into the hungry, stanky flank.

The God Slime's ravenous jelly ate through the aluminum, and suddenly its innards started blistering, bubbling, foaming. The caustic salts bloomed whitely inside the green, translucent flesh. The monster thrashed, melting faster than a sugar witch in a rainstorm, hissing a song that was pure delight to the heroes and ghosts listening, rejoicing in the vanquished catacombs.

In The Shadow of the Fryolator

EMMA LEGRASSE CRANKED the key in her Ford Festiva's ignition a third time, to no avail. She stared through the smeared windshield at the snow-blanketed hood and entertained a fleeting daydream of a sweet frosted fairyland ruled by a benevolent Jelly Donut King. Dismissing her snacky fancy, she opened her cell phone and called her boyfriend.

"Yo," answered Benny, far too loudly. She could hear him typing furiously. A dragon roared through his computer speakers. "'Sup, Em?"

"Hi, honey, my car won't start—"

"More DoTs! More DoTs! Don't go near the whelps, dumbass!" Benny screamed in her ear. Through the ringing she heard a fireball whoosh and a computerized female voice groan in death. "What an *idiot*! Uh, whadja say?"

"My car. Won't start. I'm kinda stranded here at the diner. Could you come pick me up, please? "

"Sure, I guess, after the raid," he replied, his voice flush with indifference.

"*After*?" The darned raids lasted forever. There wasn't a bus, and a cab would be at least $50. She

87

wouldn't get home until after midnight. "Honey, *please*, I've been cooking for 10 hours straight, and I've got to be back here at 8 a.m.—"

"Em, we've gotten wiped in this dungeon *twice* ... we gotta take Zirconia out this time! I'm tanking; I *can't* leave now! Look, I'll see you later. Gimme a call if you catch a ride or somethin'."

The line went dead. Emma managed to resist smashing her cell phone against the dashboard in frustration. Heaven forbid she ever got pregnant from his Mountain Dew-addled sperm – she'd have to call a cab if she went into labor on a game night.

Why do I put up with this? she wondered, then almost immediately heard the echoes of her mother's lectures that a girl had to have a man in her life, that men weren't perfect, that a good girl made do with what she got.

Criminy. Benny was preferable to her mother's hand-wringing and dire tales about the fate of single women. If Emma reported a breakup, her mother inevitably brought up the urban legend about the elderly woman who was devoured by rats the day after her divorce. That story *never* got old.

She dropped the phone and her car keys back in her purse and rubbed her numb hands on her black pants, staring balefully at the snowy hood. Cars weren't rocket science, no matter what her ex-boyfriend from Flint had tried to convince her. Changing a spark plug was easier than building a computer – which she had done, thankyouverymuch – or even just making a really good risotto.

Emma yanked the hood release and heaved the door open. The mucus in her nose froze with her first breath, and her sneaker-clad feet sank ankle-deep in the powdery snow as she went to the front of the car to wrestle the hood open. Her fingers felt like they'd been beaten with a hammer by the time she succeeded. She twisted on her keychain flashlight and examined the engine. The alternator belt hung limply on its rusty spindles, a section raggedly snapped apart. Viscous pink icicles dripped from the cold-gnawed edges of the belt. Had her transmission gone bad, too? Darn it.

Shivering, she slammed the hood shut and picked her way through the snow and icy car droppings to the back door of the Zuberoa Diner. She pushed into the warmly-lit hallway beside the cozy employee lounge, stomped the snow off her shoes, and hung her purse and coat by the door.

A weird, musky-fishy odor greased the air; she'd first noticed it around noon. She'd taken out the trash and searched the kitchen for errant sprats and prawns, to no avail. Maybe something had fallen between the counter and the fridge; she'd get one of the guys to help her pull it away from the wall if the stink persisted.

She spotted a gleaming, patterned trail of oil or slime leading from the door to the kitchen. Darn it, she'd told the busboys not to wheel their bikes through there. The tires always tracked mud and grass and who-knew-what onto the floor. Who'd be riding a bike on a day like this, anyhow? Probably Carlos; he was training for the Mountain Madness race.

Emma hurried into the kitchen to warm her aching hands against the polished insulated sides of the stainless steel Fryolator. The ghosts of French fries

IN THE SHADOW OF THE FRYOLATOR

past filled her defrosting nostrils, and the warm, oily air stung her cheeks. The new short-order guy had forgotten the closedown checklist again and left the machine on. Oh well; she had hours to kill, so she might as well precook some fresh fries for the freezer.

Mark, one of the busboys, gave her a look of surprise as he carefully loaded the last of the dishes into the washer. He had clear blue eyes, caramel-hued hair, and always smelled like gingerbread.

"I didn't think you were still here, Miz Legrasse." He always called everybody even slightly older than him Miz or Mister. She hadn't decided if that was sweet or annoying.

"Well, I shouldn't be, but my car won't start," she replied, her face caught between a reflexive smile and a frown.

"Oh, no." His eyes widened. "I have jumper cables...."

She shook her head. "The alternator belt's toast. I could use panty hose to get myself home, if I was wearing any. You don't have any, do you?"

He blinked, shuffled his feet, turned a little pink. "No, ma'am, I don't. May I give you a ride home?"

She paused, gazing at the lean muscles in his smooth forearms. He looked like he ought to be a tennis pro serving aces in the Australian sun, or modeling tight jeans under hot lights, not hauling dirty dishes in a Cleveland diner that pretended to be Basque but mostly served the same Panerafied sandwiches and pasta you'd find at any casual restaurant chain.

Mark seemed to be the most beautiful, polite, considerate, gosh-darned *charming* guy she'd ever met.

There *had* to be something horribly, horribly wrong with him. Benny, after all, never once called her "ma'am" or "miz" and tooted out a silent-but-deadly on their second date.

Mark's sweet, innocent face was surely a mask for a serial killer.

Or another Laird of Warmongrel fanatic.

"Thank you, but my boyfriend said he'd get me," she replied.

"Oh." Mark still looked concerned. "Are you sure you'll be okay here by yourself? I don't live far from here … please take my phone number, just in case."

Mark wrote his number in neat print on a yellow Post-It, said goodbye and went out to his Jeep. Emma folded the note sticky-side in and stuck it in her pants pocket. After he pulled out of the parking lot, she locked the doors and hauled one of the tall stools from the bar into the kitchen. The heck with standing to cook; she'd been on her feet most of the day and her arches were killing her.

She suddenly remembered her mother cupping her pink heels when she was a little girl, telling her she had beautiful feet, feet like a ballerina. Emma roomed with a real ballerina in college and learned that dancers' feet were cracked and callused. While Emma was at class, the ballerina ate all the Krispy Kremes and denied it afterward, as if her poor battered feet slipped out of bed at night and somehow devoured the donuts on their own.

Emma smiled at the thought of the dancer's wayward feet, then frowned, imagining a world in which that could really happen. With her luck, one day she'd wake up to find nothing but stumps underneath her own sheets and an awkward toe-scrawled "Dear Emma" letter on her nightstand.

Benny probably wouldn't bother to give her a note if he ever decided to dump her, just another monosyllabic message on her voicemail. Or maybe she wouldn't hear anything at all. Jerk.

She pushed the barstool up to the counter that held the wide maple cutting board, got a huge colander down from one of the pot racks, and opened the potato bin.

A glistening, cucumber-sized gray squid with huge parsley-colored eyes sat on top of the tubers, gazing up at her moistly.

"Greetings!" it declared in a voice like a blast from a trumpet half-filled with goo.

She gave a little shout, leaped back and grabbed the nearest kitchen implement, hoping for a knife but coming up with lobster tongs. She brandished the tongs as if they were Excalibur.

"Do not fear," said the squid, scrambling nimbly from the bin to address her from atop the cutting board. It stood up on gray frog legs, the cascade of tentacles from its face and neck obscuring anything that might grow between them. Two manlike arms emerged from the fleshy ropes and shrugged them aside; the squid-thing clasped its hands over its tentacle-draped belly and bowed to her. "I traveled many leagues and searched for many years to find you, Princess."

"P-princess?" she stammered. "W-what the heck are you?"

"I am H'telred, incarnation of the Great and Terrible God Beast of the Deeps," he declared, gripping his tentacles with one hand and raising the other doll-sized arm in a salute. "I am the heir apparent to the throne of Y'harneth, our greatest city nestled briny depths of the Esoteric Trench. But I cannot take my place as ruler until I find my princess, my queen, the only living terrestrial descendant of our resplendent lord and master, Papa Nogad.

"*You* are that descendant, fair Emma Legrasse, and you are destined for far greater things than mere mortal minds can grasp!"

Nothing was ever as nice as the stories she'd read as a little girl. Her Prince Charming had finally arrived, and he was beyond froggy. "W-what kind of things?"

"Well. You know. Queenly things." H'telred snagged a nearby red onion with one of his tentacles and used it as a stool. "Being waited on hand and fluke, drinking cosmic wines, enjoying the spoils of a conquered, subjugated Earth—"

"You're going to conquer the Earth?" She felt dizzy.

"But of course." He stood up and flourished his tentacles grandly. "I find my princess, take her as my queen, take the throne, mass my undersea armies, take over the planet, and rule over everything as a living god. It's all right there in the Books of Prophecy," he added matter-of-factly.

"Aren't you a little small for global domination?"

He flared his gills at her. "I am precisely the correct size at all times! In my natural state I'd be taller than this building. I merely shrunk myself down in the

Astigmatic Eye of Hydron. Our minions in Boston advised me that the shipping charges would become prohibitive otherwise."

"Shipping?"

"Yes, in lobster boxes. I arrived here today in one. A nice spongy bed of seaweed and some limpets to snack on – it's quite a comfy way to travel."

She crossed her arms over her apron, tongs held loosely in her left hand. "So about this queen thing – am I supposed to live in the ocean?"

His tentacles bounced as he shook his torpedo-shaped head. "We can rule the world and all its seas from this fair city. The Books of Prophecy say that Cleveland is destined to rise as the center of power of the universe and gleam like a sanguine diamond over the slave cities that fall before the arcane power of our aquatic armies."

"How's *that* going to work? We're nowhere near the coast," she pointed out.

H'telred sighed. "First we'll raise an army in Lake Erie, and then we'll invade Canada so the engineering minions can widen the Saint Lawrence River – look, we've spent *centuries* planning this. I have the overtime stubs to prove it."

H'telred blinked his nictitating membranes thoughtfully and gazed through the open door of the employee lounge. "Ah, excellent, there is a couch, and it is leather. I do despise tweed." He cleared his throat, turned toward her and knelt on one sticky knee. "Princess, I have spent aeons searching for you, and I do admit I am eager to take you as my queen so that I may plow your carnal fields and you may begin to spawn the first of many generations of fierce—"

"Wait, you want to plow my — *you want to have sex with me?*" Her voice rose to a pitch only dogs could hear.

"Yes. On that couch. Soon would be good."

"Um, not just no, but *heck* no!"

"Princess," he pleaded. "Until I'm back to my natural size, you'll hardly know I'm there. Think of your destiny. Think of the power, the riches. Think of the sushi."

He got down on both knees and clasped his hands. "Consider your adopted city. Can't you just lie back and think of Cleveland?"

"Well, mother raised me Republican ... so I guess in *theory* I might be okay with subjugating the Earth ... but I need to know that I'll still have ... *stuff.*"

"Name your heart's desires, and they shall be granted!"

"Um." Suddenly faced with listing the things dearest to her, she found her mind as desolate as the salt marshes of an abandoned fishing town. "What about my mother? I don't think she'll approve of this."

"We shall slay her together."

"No! Well ... *no.* I want her to be ... *happy.* Yes."

"Then our minions shall take her to the Space-Colored Caves, and there she shall slumber and experience a life of joy and peace inside a comforting cocoon of dreams."

"I guess that sounds good ... but what about my cat?"

"He shall be welcomed as the ambassador of a mighty predatory species. And he shall have fish."

"What about ice cream?"

"Ice cream gives cats the runs. I'd be against it."

"I mean, will there *be* ice cream?"

"Of course. The minions have a fondness for Antarctica Bars and Cool Air Swirls."

Suddenly, an idea emitted a keening croak from the marsh of her mind. "What about *Star Trek*?"

"Indeed, it has been cancelled, and for good reason, but you shall have every frame of *Star Trek* ever recorded–"

"No, I want *new Star Trek*. I want *more*. I want it to be *good*."

He twitched his tentacles. "That, I'm afraid, isn't doable. After they've served their purpose during the propaganda phase, we shall invite every actor, director and producer to private awards banquets and slaughter them to feed the shogg–"

"I am totally not having sex with you if I don't get new *Star Trek*." She put her hands on her hips.

"Princess, be reasonable! Surely you would not turn down your destiny over this! What has the television industry ever done for you? They've insulted mighty Cleveland, scorned this beautiful Forest City, mocked the fair state of Ohio again and again! Hollywood's used your people as the butt of jokes because they cravenly fear to offend the well-armed denizens of the American South. How could you, a Princess from The Queen City–"

"Cincinnati? I'm from Kansas City."

"Kansas City?" He pulled a tiny leather-bound tome from beneath his tentacles and opened it. "Your mother's name is Sandy Lumley, is it not?"

"Uh, no, her name's Edith."

"Oh." H'telred closed the book carefully. "It seems there has been an error, and I have found the wrong Emma Legrasse. Well. I need to consult the white pages. And the Mapquest. Does yon lounge hold a computer?"

"Not anymore, the waiters kept downloading por—wait, you're saying I'm *not* the princess?"

"Alas, no. You are destined merely for gibbering slavery. And I come now to regret taking pains to keep

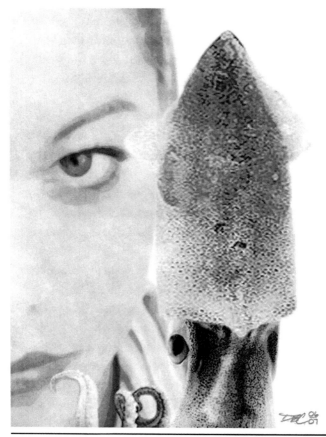

you here after hours, for now I must seek the Internets at Starbucks and you cannot carry me hence—"

"Taking pains?" She stared at the pink saliva dripping from his tiny, toothed maw and remembered the icicles on her broken alternator belt. "You sabotaged my car?"

"Well, the cold did make it rather painful to chew—"

The proverbial last straw broke inside her with the snap of tiny slimy neckbones.

"Rat bastard son of a bitch!" she exclaimed, then grabbed him with the tongs, and dumped him into the nearest vat of 250-degree oil in the Fryolator. H'telred gave out a split-second shriek before he burst in a jet of stinky steam. A gray slick of liquefied fat spread across the bubbling oil.

Damn. I'm going to have to completely drain the pan and scrub it out, she thought, dazed, watching the oil curdle to loathsome mayonnaise around his crisping tentacles.

Chilly realizations dawned on her. She'd just turned a tyrannical mini-demigod into very bad calamari. And he had royal minions. His freakish fish-men would surely seek dire vengeance on her once they discovered she'd popped their master.

But more important, she'd actually considered marrying a squid! What had gotten into her?

Well, most any attention from H'telred was bound to be more interesting than what she'd been getting. She stared at the tiny suckers curling into hard brown balls. Yep, sex with squidboy couldn't have been worse than Benny.

Dammit. She'd almost been a princess. She'd almost been queen of the world. Her mother would never believe it. Emma stared down at her cold, aching feet. Feet that her mother promised the pink silk of ballerinadom … but denied actual dance lessons.

Something hardened inside Emma like a French fry left too long in the vat. H'telred started to smoke. She fished him out with the tongs, doused his crackling corpse with cold water and dumped it in the trash. Screw her mother's old wives tales. Screw years of waiting for cold frogs to turn into hot princes. She fetched her phone and called Benny.

"We're not finished yet–" he began.

"Yes, we are," she replied. "You're a nearly useless human being and a crappy boyfriend. I never want to see you again. Goodbye." She hit the "end" button fiercely and deleted his entry.

She pulled out Mark's Post-It and began to punch in his number. A serial killer might have practical ideas on how to dispatch fishy thugs. And if he was just a genuinely sweet kid working his way through school – well, she sure could use a ride home.

Another hand to clean the damn Fryolator wouldn't hurt, either.

Author's Acknowledgements

I would like to thank the editors who gave me suggestions on these stories: Brit Marshalk and Eugie Foster of *The Town Drunk*, and David L. Duggins of *Spacesuits and Sixguns*. Very special thanks go to Kyle Niedzwiecki and David Horwich of *Strange Horizons;* their input really got the ball rolling on these stories. And of course I'd like to thank Pete S. Allen for publishing this collection, and to thank Malcolm McClinton and D.E. Christman for their artwork. Last but not least, I'd like to thank my husband, Gary A. Braunbeck, for his love and support.

The following stories in this collection were previously published:

- "Installing Linux on a Dead Badger: User's Notes" – *Strange Horizons*, April 5, 2004.

- "Your Corporate Network and the Forces of Darkness" – *Strange Horizons*, June 20, 2005.

- "Faery Cats: The Cutest Killers" – *Strange Horizons*, February 27, 2006.

- "Graveyard Shift" – *The Town Drunk*, November 2006:
  - "Dead Men Don't Need Coffee Breaks"
  - "Business Insourcing Offers Life After Death"
  - "Corporate Vampires Sink Teeth Into Business World"
  - "Unemployed Playing Dead To Find Work"

- "Authorities Concerned Over Rise of Teen Linux Gangs" – *The Town Drunk*, December 2006.

- "Wake Up Naked Monkey You're Going To Die" – *Horror World*, March 2007.

- "The Great VüDü Teen Linux Zombie Massacree" – *Spacesuits and Sixguns*, Spring 2007.

About the Author

LUCY A. SNYDER grew up in the cowboys-and-cactus part of Texas. Although the kids got a school holiday whenever the rodeo came to town, young Lucy yearned to live in a land that featured more seasons and fewer cases of sunstroke. Her first attempts at poetry were inspired by the escape of her beloved pet tarantula during a 4th grade field trip:

> *I had a big fuzzy spider*
> *I named him Mister Squizzy*
> *He got loose on the schoolbus*
> *He's not in your lunchbox, is he?*

Still fascinated with spiders as an adult, she earned a BS in biology and intended to become a scientist. Unfortunately, she discovered in her senior year that she was horrifically bad at electrophoresis. Still determined to experience autumn and spring, she moved to Bloomington, Indiana to get her MA in journalism. She figured that if she couldn't do science, at least she could write about it in newspapers and magazines. Soon after she moved into the dorm, she made her first science fiction short story sale.

Thrilled, she rededicated herself to fiction writing, and two years later she got into the Clarion Science Fiction & Fantasy Writers' Workshop in East Lansing, Michigan. At Clarion, she learned a great deal about plot, characterization, and the importance of keeping business receipts. But near the end of the workshop, she made the mistake of turning in a funny fantasy story. The instructor that week began his evaluation of her tale thusly: "This story represents everything that's wrong with the science fiction and fantasy being written today…"

His criticism didn't get kinder. Afterward, Lucy naturally figured that humor was right up there with electrophoresis on the list of things she should never try again. So, she spent the next few years designing web sites, editing for various online magazines, and trying to write the best, most serious speculative fiction she possibly could.

That changed in 2002 when she discovered an odd site called Everything2.com. At E2, she discovered she could write about pretty much any weird thing that popped into her head, and she would find an interested audience for it there. Setting aside concerns about producing sellable stories, Lucy began to experiment with forms of writing that were completely new to her.

In early 2004, an E2 user posted instructions for installing Linux on an extremely obsolete piece of hardware. In the site's chat room, another user sarcastically commented, "What's he going to do next, tell us how to install Linux on a dead badger?"

Lucy, who'd been reading reams of bad technical documentation for her web design jobs, was much amused by the notion. How *would* you install Linux on a dead badger? What flavor would you use? What would a Linux-powered badger be good for?

She posted "How to Install Linux on a Dead Badger" to E2, and it quickly became a site favorite. Later, she revised the piece and sold it to the articles department at *Strange Horizons*; that expanded version got linked from the popular *Slashdot* site, resulting in a huge surge of traffic for the magazine. Even today, "Installing Linux on a Dead Badger: User's Notes" is still one of the most popular features at *SH*.

Lucy has continued to write and sell funny stories. Today, nearly half of her 40+ published short stories and many of her published essays contain elements of satire or other strong humor. Several of her non-badger humor pieces appear in her first collection, *Sparks and Shadows*, which was published by HW Press in May 2007.

For more information about Lucy, please visit:
www.lucysnyder.com

ABOUT THE AUTHOR

About the Artists

D.E. CHRISTMAN is an artist who simply wants to scare the hell out of you. And he takes great pleasure in doing so. His Lovecraftian inspired work has been described as "Twisted, demented and wonderfully creepy" (*The Horror-Web*), a description he takes great pride in. His art has been featured an many galleries, art shows, magazines, book covers, and websites that specialize in the macabre and strange.

He makes his living through his company Grendel's Den Design Studio, producing art and design for print and web. He is also regarded as one of Philadelphia's premier zombie experts and has given various interviews and lectures regarding his knowledge of both the living dead and slaves of the famous voodoo curse.

For more information about D.E., please visit:
www.grendelsden.net

MALCOLM MCCLINTON has been drawing and painting science fiction and fantasy subjects as long as he can remember. But until nine years ago, illustrating was only a hobby, something he would do to relax. Most of his efforts had been in academia, where he earned advanced degrees in physical anthropology and archaeology. But after spending five or six years laboring at excavation sites, he burned out and subsequently took a job at Dark Horse Comics doing production work.

This career change reignited his creative drive and after three years he left to pursue his own painting and projects. He has been illustrating as a means of making a living ever since. He has created a nice little niche for himself that satisfies his natural anti-authoritarianism, his reclusive nature and his need for adulation all at once.

For more information about Malcolm, please visit: hanged-man.deviantart.com